CHICAGO
THE GROWTH OF THE CITY

CHICAGO

THE GROWTH OF THE CITY

CHARTWELL
BOOKS, INC.

This edition published in 2007 by

CHARTWELL BOOKS, INC.
A Division of
BOOK SALES, INC.
114 Northfield Avenue
Edison, New Jersey 08837

ISBN-13: 978-0-7858-2214-1
ISBN-10: 0-7858-2214-3

© 2007 Compendium Publishing, 43 Frith Street, London,
Soho, W1V 4SA, United Kingdom

Cataloging-in-Publication data is available from the Library
of Congress

Printed and bound in China

Design: Ian Hughes/Compendium Design

Page 2: A view over downtown Chicago, clustered around the
Chicago River as it has been since the earliest days of the city.
Page 4: The clock outside Marshall Field's is one of Chicago's best-
loved landmarks.

Contents

Introduction

As you might expect from a city that pioneered the skyscraper, the Chicago skyline is made up hundreds of towers, designed in a myriad of innovative architectural styles. Still one of the United States' most dynamic cities, Chicago is also famed as a center of art, music, and learning as well as for its colorful history.

Introduction

At the southern tip of Lake Michigan, in the state of Illinois, is the United States' "second city." The crucible of American modern architecture and long-time rival to New York, Chicago is now actually the third-largest city in North America, but in terms of architectural and cultural influence it stands as tall as any in the world. The hub of transportation for the United States', home to some of the most impressive skyscrapers in the world, and as dynamic today as at any point during its explosively successful history, Chicago has grown from inauspicious, muddy beginnings into one of the globe's most exciting cities.

The area that Chicago now occupies was named by its original inhabitants, Algonquin speaking tribes who called it *Checaugou*, which translates as either "skunk cabbage" or "wild onion," and referred to the vegetable smells rising from the damp, marshy land. Even then, the Native-Americans hereabouts enjoyed excellent communication with tribes to the north, south, and east, a fact that didn't escape early explorers who also noted the short portage between what would be named the Chicago River, which flowed into the Great Lakes system, and the Des Plaines River that joined the Mississippi.

The first people of European extraction to pass through the area were the missionary Jacques Marquette and the explorer Louis Jolliet, who arrived in 1673, made basic maps of the area, and

This montage of illustrations entitled "Chicago in Early Days 1779-1856" shows the growth of Chicago from the first cabin built by Jean Baptiste Pointe DuSable (top row, second image on the left) to a thriving metropolis. Below is a key to each image (from left to right, top to bottom): 1. Old Fort Dearborn, 1803; 2. The First Cabin, 1779, Built by Jean Baptiste Point de Saible; 3. Chicago, 1845; 4. First Rush Medical College, 1837; 5. Fort Dearborn, 1816; 6. The First Court House, 1835; 7. Water Works, 1853; 8. Chicago, 1830; 9. Wolf Point, 1830; 10. Clybourne House; 11. Green Tree Hotel, 1833; 12. Old Kinzie Mansion, 1832; 13. Chicago, 1853; 14. Sauganash Hotel, 1831; 15. Old Block House and Light House, 1857.

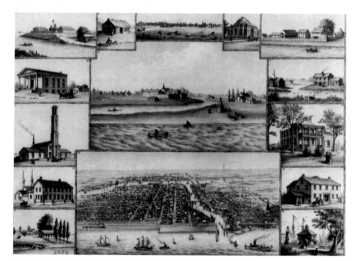

noted the tribes' name for the land. They were followed by numerous other traders and explorers, but it was not until 1683 that an attempt was made at settlement. The first Europeans to set up home here were French Jesuits who built the Fort de Chicago in 1683. In 1696, Francois Pinet opened the Mission of the Guardian Angel, which lasted only four years, the local tribes proving resistant to Christian conversion. By 1705, the fort, too, was abandoned when hostility between the local tribe and French traders flared up. In fact, it was over a century after Marquette and Jolliet's visit that the first successful non-native settler arrived. Jean-Baptiste Pointe du Sable was an African-American from Haiti and the home that he set up with his Native-American wife on the north bank at the mouth of the Chicago River marked the real beginning of Chicago's story. The few reports that we have of the city's founder describe him as a refined man of many skills; nevertheless his homestead was an isolated settlement until 1795 when, under the Treaty of Greenville, the Native-American tribes ceded six square miles of land at the mouth of the Chicago River to the United States. A few years later, in 1803, the United States Army built Fort Dearborn to protect the fledgling town's new settlers, not only from incursions by local tribes, but from the French and British. Although the fort was destroyed during the War of 1812, it was rebuilt in 1816 and continued to preside over the tiny town until 1837. At the time of its construction few would have predicted Chicago's later success. Indeed, by 1830 it is estimated that the population was barely a hundred hardy souls, living on boggy land that was plagued by disease-carrying insects.

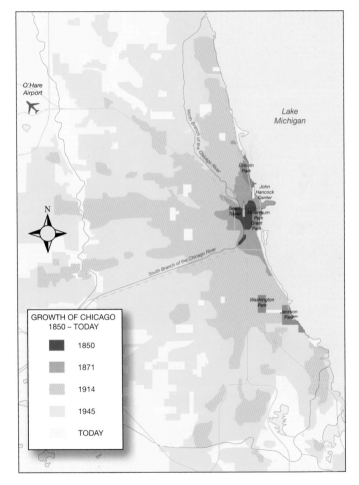

GROWTH OF CHICAGO
1850 – TODAY

1850
1871
1914
1945
TODAY

Despite the less than hospitable landscape, during the 1830s the settlement's fortunes began to improve. With the completion of the Erie Canal linking New York City to Lake Erie in 1825, colonization of the West began to gather pace, and, like many other small settlements, Chicago benefited, particularly as the government were selling off interests in the future Illinois and Michigan Canal. Incorporated as a town in 1833 with a population of 350, Chicago received its city charter just four years later, and by the end of the decade boasted over 4,000 residents. It was in the latter half of the next decade, however, that Chicago had the first taste of its future success. In 1848, the Illinois and Michigan Canal opened, joining the Chicago River at Bridgeport to the Illinois River at LaSalle. Now cargo could navigate a route from New York (by now the nation's leading port) through the Great Lakes to the Gulf of Mexico for the first time. Poised in the center and trading furiously in both directions was Chicago. In the same year the city welcomed its first rail line, the Galena & Chicago Railroad and the Board of Trade was set up by Chicago merchants. Transportation and trade was to prove the key to success. Chicago soon eclipsed St. Louis as the hub of Midwestern commerce and by 1850 its population had rocketed to nearly 30,000. This was, however, just the beginning. Within thirty years the relatively small city would have a population of over half a million and become, next to New York, the second largest city in the United States and one of the biggest in the world. During these three decades railroads proliferated. By 1860 Chicago's rail terminals served fifteen operators, who were spreading their steel web ever further across the continent.

This illustration is probably some way from being an accurate representation of Chicago in 1831, yet it does show that a settlement is beginning to grow. By now Chicago's population would have been about a hundred, housed in homesteads close to the fort.

Not drawn to scale, this panoramic view of Chicago was published in 1857. In the twenty-six years since the preceding illustration the settlement has become a fully-fledged city. Note the heavy water traffic on the Chicago River as boats head upstream toward the recently opened Illinois and Michigan Canal, which would take them on to the Mississippi and eventually to the Gulf of Mexico. Ships headed in the opposite direction are destined for New York via the Erie Canal. Just to the left of the river close to the lake shore is the passenger depot of the Illinois Central Rail Road and the Michigan Central Rail Road, surrounded by freight depots and railroad offices. By this time Chicago was the transport hub of the United States.

A similar view to the previous illustration, this panoramic map shows Chicago in 1868, just ten years later. The city's continued rapid growth is evident in the spread of the commercial district further back from the river on both banks.

This scene of the Great Fire of Chicago in 1871 shows Chicagoans fleeing across the Randolph Street Bridge. The fire eventually razed almost all of the downtown area, but prepared the way for the city's most energetic and ambitious period of growth and expansion.

As the population increased and wealth flooded into Chicago, the city that was at the time notorious as being the dirtiest in America started to improve it infrastructure, most importantly lifting itself out of the mud between 1855 and 1858. This monumental engineering feat involved laying sewer pipes above ground. Each building was then jacked up and soil used to raise the street level by between four and seven feet, creating an underground sewage system while simultaneously raising Chicago. Mercy Hospital, the first in Illinois, also began treating the city's sick in 1863, while 1867 saw work begin on one of Chicago's most famous landmarks, W.W. Boyington's Water Tower.

In 1871, disaster struck. Local legend has it that a cow belonging to a Mrs. O'Leary kicked a lantern, thus starting the Great Chicago Fire. Whether or not the cow was responsible, the fire spread from the O'Leary barn and raged through Chicago for thirty-six hours from October 8th to 10th, razing the city's downtown area, most of which was constructed of wood, almost entirely. Over 18,000 buildings were destroyed, 300 killed, and a third of the city's 300,000 people rendered homeless.

While the Great Fire was undoubtedly a civic catastrophe, it effectively ended the first phase of Chicago's development and cleared the ground for a new era of even more explosive growth. In fact, the city recovered from the Great Fire with breathtaking rapidity. Although times were politically turbulent, reaching a nadir with the Haymarket Riot of 1886, the next thirty years would see the city's population expand from a more-than-respectable 300,000 to an astounding 1.7 million, making it the fastest growing metropolis in recorded history. It was also becoming increasingly sophisticated. By 1879, the Art Institute had been founded and in 1890 the University of Chicago came into existence with a donation from John D. Rockefeller. In 1892, the elevated tramway (or the "L") opened, moving commuters around downtown. Along the way, Chicago's audacious rebuild nurtured the talents of some of America's foremost architects, such as Daniel H. Burnham, John Welbourne Root, Dankmar Adler, Louis Sullivan, and William Le Baron Jenney. With the design of the Home Insurance Building of 1884, the latter introduced the world to what is considered the first skyscraper. Chicago took something of a shine to the tall building and decided that a few more would not look out of place. Buildings such as The Rookery (1888) and the Reliance Building (1895) were at the cutting edge of a revolution in architecture that became known as the Chicago School. As the century drew to a close a young man by the name of Frank Lloyd Wright arrived in the city and entered the employ of Adler and Sullivan's firm. He would go on to become America's most famous architect and bestow on Chicago some of his most significant works.

The final decade of the nineteenth century also saw Chicago take center stage with the World's Columbian Exposition of 1893, generally considered the greatest World's Fair ever held. Built on reclaimed land, the grounds were landscaped by Frederick Law Olmsted, of Central Park fame, and its Classically-themed buildings and pavilions raised by a team of the nation's finest architects under the guidance of Daniel Burnham. During the six

Chicago in 1892. The water between the Illinois Central Rail Road Tracks and Michigan Avenue has been filled in to create Grant Park (then known as Lake Park).

The large building in the park is the Interstate Exposition Building, built in 1871 as the city's first convention center. The new harbor also dates to the same year.

months it was open, nearly twenty-eight million people passed through its gates.

The twentieth century began for Chicago with an engineering feat of stupendous scope. The Chicago Sanitary and Ship Canal reversed the flow of the Chicago River, which meant that it would now carry the city's effluence away from Lake Michigan (the source of the city's drinking water). The population also continued to swell, and was increasingly augmented by African-American migrants from the South as the first decade passed. Seeking work in the city's factories, Chicago's newest settlers generally headed for the "Black Belt" on the South Side and brought with them the new musical styles of Jazz and blues that Chicago would become so famous for in the 1920s. They joined European immigrants, notably the Irish who had been arriving since the potato famine of the 1840s as well as Greeks, Czechs, Poles, and Italians who had been streaming into the city since the 1870s. By 1930, Chicago's citizens numbered 3,376,438 and the city was home to a huge diversity of races and cultures. While this was not always a comfortable mixture (as witnessed during the Race Riots of 1919), the city had by now developed a unique personality that was greater than the sum of its parts. It had also built many much-loved landmarks, such as Navy Pier (1916), Wrigley Building (1924), the

Tribune Tower (1925), Merchandise Mart (1930), Adler Planetarium (1930), and Shedd Aquarium (1930). The modern city was also served by its first airfield—The Chicago Municipal Airport (since renamed Midway Airport) opened in 1927—had straightened the Chicago River to make way for further downtown expansion in 1928, and become synonymous with the culture of speakeasies, jazz, and—more unfortunately—organized crime, as personified by Mafia boss Al Capone who arrived in 1919 and was not gaoled until 1931.

In 1933, Chicago opened another World's Fair, this time dedicated to invention and innovation, an appropriate theme for such a dynamic city. Close to forty million people would visit during the two seasons it was open. While the city suffered along with the rest of the United States during the Great Depression, its recovery was rapid and complete; soon after the end of World War II, the city's population had reached an all time high of just under 3.7 million. For much of the remainder of the twentieth century the number of people in Chicago would dwindle as citizens served by excellent public transport links and motor cars headed out into the suburbs. The result was a number of impoverished neighborhoods. Nevertheless, Chicago continued to make improvements and erect grand new buildings over the second half of twentieth century, notably opening O'Hare Airport to take the strain from Midway, which was the world's busiest airport by the mid-fifties, as well as building four major expressways during the office of Mayor Richard J. Daley and capturing the title of world's tallest building when Sears Tower was completed in 1973. As the

LEFT: The World's Columbian Exposition of 1893 marked the 400th anniversary of Christopher Columbus's discovery of the American continent with the construction of an incredible complex of Classical-inspired exhibition buildings that became known as the "White City." Unfortunately, few of these architectural wonders have survived.

twentieth century progressed toward its end the city also elected its first female and African-American mayors (Jane M. Byrne in 1979 and Harold Washington in 1983). As the millennium dawned Chicago was celebrating a recent upturn in it population, which was breathing new life into many neglected areas. It also opened Millennium Park in 2004, a fitting tribute to a city with a reputation as one of the world's leading centers of architectural excellence.

This book presents a pictorial history of Chicago's growth and development. Obviously, a subject so vast cannot be covered comprehensively in any one volume, but we hope that these images convey a sense of how Chicago has evolved into such a unique and special place.

ABOVE: This 1926 illustration of the Chicago skyline shows the city's buildings reaching higher. To the far right of the picture are the Wrigley Building (1922) and Tribune Tower (1925). The Metropolitan Tower (1924) is in the foreground to the left of center.

RIGHT: A view over Chicago and the Century of Progress Exposition, built for the 1933 World's Fair. In the foreground is the Field Museum of Natural History (1921) with the circular Shedd Aquarium (1930) to the right.

FOLLOWING PAGE: This more recent panoramic photograph of Chicago's skyline is dominated by the sleek, black Sears Tower (1974) to the left of the photograph. At the right of center is the white monolith of Aon Center (1973) to the left of which is Two Prudential Plaza (1990). Since the Home Insurance Building introduced Chicago to the skyscraper in 1884, over 1,000 high-rise buildings of over nine floors have been erected in the city and more are planned. At the time of going to press a 2,000-foot twisted spire is being planned. If construction goes ahead it will open at 400 North Lake Shore in 2009.

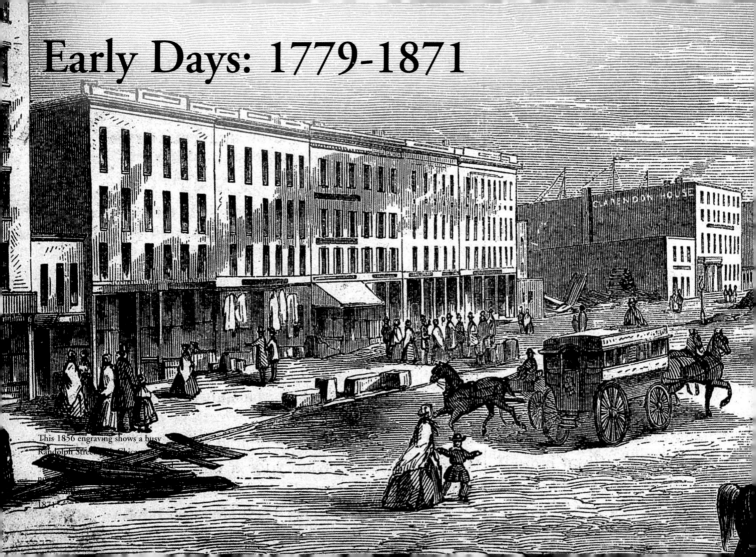

Early Days: 1779-1871

This 1856 engraving shows a busy
Randolph Street in Chicago

Early Days: 1779-1871

While the area that Chicago now occupies was first visited by Europeans in the late seventeenth century, it was not until 1779, that the first successful non-Native-American settler arrived and built a small settlement that would eventually blossom as one of the world's greatest—and richest—cities. Initially growth was slow. In fact, Jean Baptiste du Sable's house also served all civic functions; it was here that Chicago's first marriage took place as well as its first election. Nevertheless, more pioneers gradually trickled in and by 1803 they were joined by the garrison of Fort Dearborn, built across the river to protect settlers and trade. Standing, as it did, over the Chicago portage, the fort soon became one of the nation's most important trading posts. Nevertheless, outside its walls Chicago consisted of only a handful of log cabins until the 1830s when work began on providing Chicago with a harbor and lighthouse. As trade increased so to did the population, jumping from about 100 in 1830 to 4,470 by the beginning of the next decade, by which time Chicago was an officially incorporated city. The population increased sharply again throughout the next decade as work commenced on making Chicago a water link in the transportation route between the Gulf of Mexico and New York City. On completion in 1848, the Illinois and Michigan Canal spurred the city on to even more rapid growth, which was quickened further by the arrival of the railroad. Indeed, as the mid-century arrived, Chicago's population had multiplied to just under 30,000, railroad lines and terminals proliferated, Chicago's harbor bristled with the masts of ships, and commercial buildings sprang up along the banks of the Chicago River, particularly in the downtown area. By 1865, the city was the home of the world's largest stockyard and its streets stretched for miles beyond downtown as buildings were hastily erected to house the tens of thousands of new arrivals streaming into the city. Unfortunately, the rough and ready building was to prove the city's undoing. In 1871, the population that now numbered almost 300,000 witnessed a catastrophic fire that laid waste to its downtown heart.

This illustration, titled "Chicago in 1820" actually dates to the 1850s. Although it is unlikely to be an accurate depiction of the early settlement it does show Fort Dearborn, rebuilt after the War of 1812 (to the south of the river) and the tiny village founded by Jean-Baptiste Pointe du Sable.

Seen here surrounded by signs of progress and prosperity in 1856, Fort Dearborn (LEFT) was built in 1803 across the river from the cabin built by Jean Baptiste Pointe DuSable in 1779 and stood over the entry to the Chicago Portage. Destroyed during the War of 1812 following an uprising of Potawatomi, it was rebuilt in 1816 and remained for another forty years. In 1928 a monument was erected (RIGHT AND BELOW) at the site of the fort commemorating the pioneers who discovered Chicago and those who died at the hands of the Potawatomi in the Fort Dearborn Massacre.

DEFENSE

FORT DEARBORN STOOD ALMOST ON THIS SPOT. AFTER AN HEROIC DEFENSE IN EIGHTEEN HUNDRED AND TWELVE THE GARRISON TOGETHER WITH WOMEN AND CHILDREN WAS FORCED TO EVACUATE THE FORT LED FORTH BY CAPTAIN WELLS. THEY WERE BRUTALLY MASSACRED BY THE INDIANS THEY WILL BE CHERISHED AS MARTYRS IN OUR EARLY HISTORY

ERECTED BY THE TRUSTEES OF THE B.F. FERGUSON MONUMENT FUND 1928

LEFT: The Classical Revival-style Clarke House is the city's oldest surviving building. Dating to 1836, it was built by Henry and Caroline Clarke on twenty acres on Sixteenth Street and Michigan Avenue, but was moved to the Prairie Avenue Historic District in 1977. Sadly, none of its original furnishings remain, but it has been carefully refurbished to recreate the original style and now operates as a museum of middle-class life in early Chicago.

RIGHT: To the southwest of the city is the Illinois and Michigan Canal National Heritage Corridor. Although the canal has not been used commercially since being superseded by the Illinois Waterway in 1933, in 1984 it was designated a national heritage corridor and now features trails and camping sites along about a hundred miles of its length. At Lockport are these pioneer homes, recreated to show visitors how workers on the canal would have lived. Many laborers died of disease during the canal's construction, but when the waterway opened in 1848 it paved the way for an unparalleled period of growth in Chicago that lasted well into the next century.

Today's Lincoln Park began as a cemetery on Chicago's northern edge. In 1860, sixty acres were set aside as Lake Park, which was renamed soon after the president was assassinated in 1865.

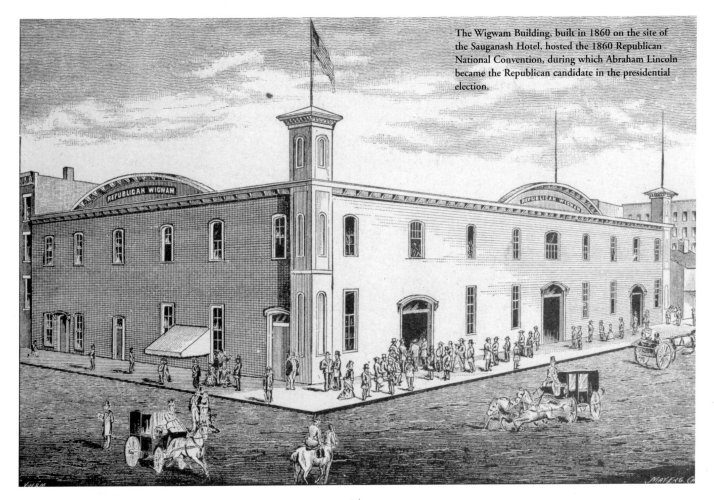

The Wigwam Building, built in 1860 on the site of the Sauganash Hotel, hosted the 1860 Republican National Convention, during which Abraham Lincoln became the Republican candidate in the presidential election.

This iron-and-wood swing bridge was built across
the Chicago River at Rush Street in 1857 and could
be rotated ninety degrees to allow passage to river
traffic. Safety procedures were non-existent and if
anyone was crossing the bridge at the time they
would be stranded on it until the ship had passed.

The Railroad Comes to Chicago

On October 10, 1848, Chicago welcomed the first locomotive to steam into the city on the newly finished Galena & Chicago Union Railroad. The first tracks ran west from the city to Clinton, Iowa, and Freeport, Illinois and allowed produce and other resources to be transported into Chicago from whence they could be shipped on to via the new Illinois and Michigan Canal. Chicago was suddenly the transport hub of the Midwest. As many more rail lines were laid and terminals completed, people and goods flooded into the city and fortunes were made.

At the time of the completion of its first line in 1856, the Illinois and Central Railroad crossed 700 miles from Chicago to the southern end of Illinois, and was the longest rail line in the world. This contemporary illustration shows a the grand facade of the railroad's terminal, which occupied a site on the south bank of the Chicago River close to Lake Michigan.

BELOW: This photograph purports to show the *Pioneer*, the first ever locomotive to arrive in Chicago in 1848.

RIGHT: This map shows the extent of the Galena & Chicago Union Railroad as well as other lines by 1862. Just fourteen years after the first line into the city opened, Chicago is at the center of an expansive network that reaches as far west as Nebraska.

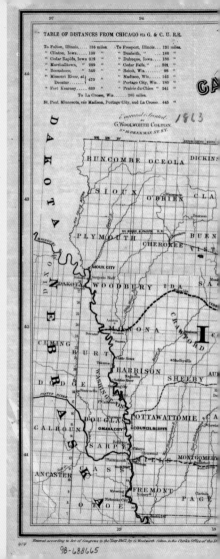

TABLE OF DISTANCES FROM CHICAGO via G. & C. U. R.R.

To Fulton, Illinois,	136 miles.	To Freeport, Illinois,	121 miles.
" Clinton, Iowa	138	" Dunleith,	183
" Cedar Rapids, Iowa	219	" Dubuque, Iowa	188
" Marshalltown,	289	" Cedar Falls,	221
" Boonsboro,	340	" Beloit, Wis.	98
" Missouri River, at }	470	" Madison, Wis.	145
" Decatur, }		" Portage City, Wis.	180
" Fort Kearney,	680	" Prairie du Chien "	241

To La Crosse, Wis. ..... 365 miles.

St. Paul, Minnesota, *via* Madison, Portage City, and La Crosse, 445 miles.

Engraved & Printed.
G. WOOLWORTH COLTON. 1863
N.º 10 BEEKMAN St N.Y.

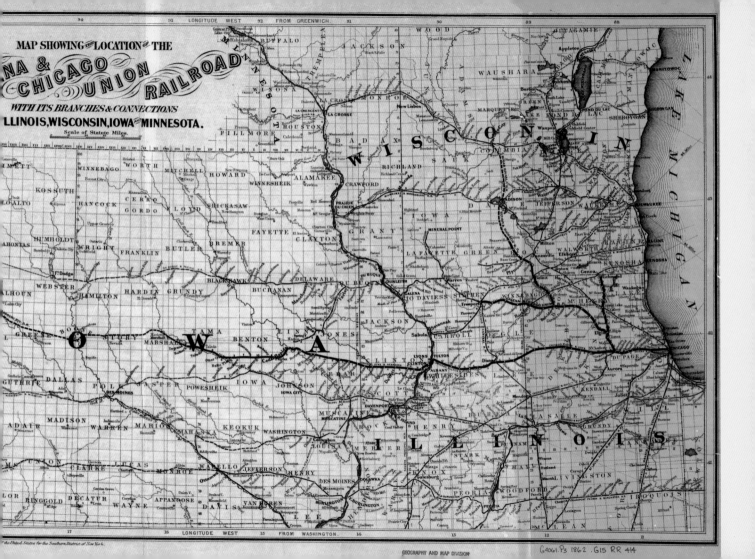

MAP SHOWING THE LOCATION OF THE
[IOW]NA & CHICAGO UNION RAILROAD
WITH ITS BRANCHES & CONNECTIONS
[I]LLINOIS, WISCONSIN, IOWA AND MINNESOTA.

Scale of Statute Miles

LEFT: By the 1860s Chicago was a thriving city with a population of over 110,000 and, as can be seen in this illustration of Randolph Street, a growing number of brick and stone buildings. Nevertheless, most of the city was still built of wood. As of 1858 the street level had also been raised, with a new sewer system in place, eliminating the city's drainage problems.

RIGHT: The Union Stock Yard & Transit Co., seen here in 1878, opened in Chicago on Christmas Day, 1865, and quickly became America's abattoir. Originally built on 320 acres in the southwest of the city (enlarged to 475 acres in 1900) by a consortium of railroad companies, the yards attracted a number of meatpacking companies, which by the beginning of the twentieth century were handling over eighty percent of all the meat eaten across the nation. Subsidiary businesses made soap, glue, polishes, and other goods from by-products, while a whole neighborhood (known locally as "Back of the Yards") grew up around it, housing more than 25,000 workers, mostly immigrants from many different parts of Europe as well as African-Americans from the South.

LEFT AND RIGHT: One of the great Chicago landmarks, Marshall Field's history began with a dry goods store opened by the legendary Potter Palmer on Lake Street in 1852. By 1867, ownership had passed to the partnership of Field and Levi Leiter, who moved into this building built by Palmer in 1868. When it was razed during the Great Fire, Field demonstrated his commitment to profit by first rescuing as much of his stock as possible from the building then opening shop in an old railroad building until new premises could be found. In 1876, the partners returned to the site of their first premises only to have the replacement building burn to the ground once more the following year. Again a temporary store was opened until the current building was completed in 1879. Field together with a number of junior partners bought Leiter out in 1881 and the store became simply Marshall Field & Co.

ABOVE: The 154-foot Water Tower and Pumping Station on North Michigan Avenue was constructed in 1869 to stabilize Chicago's mains water pressure. Designed by William W. Boyinton, these remarkable water works buildings resemble miniature Gothic castles.

The Great Chicago Fire of 1871

At roughly nine in the evening of Sunday, October 8, 1871, a fire was started in the barn behind the home of Mrs. O'Leary at 137 DeKoven Street on the West Side. Rapidly growing beyond control, within a few hours the blaze had crossed the river and become an inferno. Shortly after midnight the downtown business district was on fire and the flames were spreading to the north. The fire burned everything in its path all the following day, until it began to rain late that night. The city was devastated—300 people were dead, close to 100,000 homeless, hundreds of thousands of dollars worth of property destroyed, and millions would be lost in revenue during rebuilding. Nevertheless, within the space of a few years Chicago would be built anew; bigger, better, and taller than ever. In fact, much of the rubble would be cleared into Lake Michigan to form new land south of the river. The new Chicago would truly rise from the ashes of the old.

Taken soon after the last of the flames was doused, this panorama vividly depicts the extent of the damage. Entire streets have been completely razed and buildings made from brick and stone have fared little better. All that remains are a few blackened walls. These, too, would have to be demolished before rebuilding work could begin. It would take a number of days for the remains to cool enough to allow a detailed survey of the damage.

RIGHT: This view from the West Side shows downtown Chicago burning and citizens escaping carrying their children and valuables. To the right of the scene the Water Tower can be seen standing. It would be one of the very few structures to escape the flames.

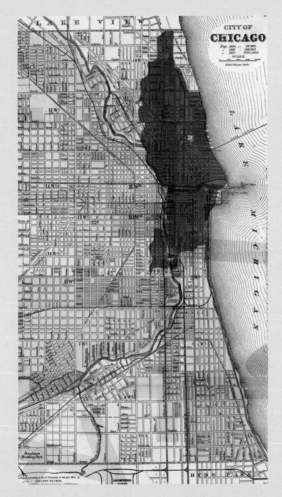

CITY OF
CHICAGO

LEFT: The bright red area
on this map shows the
portion of the city that was
burned during the fire.
Ironically, because the
wind changed direction
soon after the fire started,
Mrs. O'Leary's house
survived intact. Now
demolished, a training
academy for fire fighters
stands on the site.

RIGHT: The ruins of
Chicago's business district.
In the days after the fire it
was commonplace to see
men wielding sledge-
hammers attempting to
open the many scorched
safes that littered the area.
Trains could no longer
reach their terminals and
traffic across the river was
limited to the bridge at
Twelfth Street.

FAR RIGHT: The remains of
Trinity Episcopal Church
on Jackson Street at
Michigan and Wabash.
The congregation would
subsequently move to a
new church at Twenty-
sixth and Michigan.

The Fastest Growing City in History: 1872–1914

A panorama of Chicago in 1909, taken over the railroad yards that played such an important part in the city's meteoric rise.

The Fastest Growing City in History: 1872–1914

The decades following the fire are perhaps Chicago's most important. Where expansion had been fast before, now the Chicago's growth was more rapid than any other city in human history: the population almost doubled to half a million in the decade after the fire and by the time World War I broke out Chicago's citizens numbered well over two million. Architecturally, Chicago lead the world into a new age. The downtown area was soon cleared of rubble and new stone, steel, and glass buildings were erected. In 1884, William Le Baron Jenney created the world's first skyscraper and began to train other Chicago architects in his methods. The innovative steel frame that allowed architects to create soaring buildings free of load-bearing walls was to prove a turning point for architecture around the world, and particularly Chicago. As the new century began, Frank Lloyd Wright would also devise the Prairie Style that gave America its first home-grown architectural language and shape the look of Chicago's "Bungalow Belt." Business was booming, too, and people poured into the city at an astounding rate, including many immigrants from around the world looking for a better life for themselves and their families. The mixture of people from different social classes and cultural backgrounds undoubtedly helped give Chicago a unique and distinctive character, but in those days the divisions often lead to conflict. The influx of people saw Chicago fracture into many different neighborhoods as it grew.

Culturally, Chicago was growing too; the University of Chicago opened in 1890, welcoming students of both sexes and all races, and with the World's Columbian Exposition of 1893, Chicago took a place on the world stage and philanthropists were inspired to found

many of Chicago's present day institutions. In the summer of that year, tens of millions of people would flock to what is generally regarded as the finest world's fair in history.

Chicago began rebuilding as soon as the fire was extinguished, aided by money, food, furnishings, materials, and clothing donated by other cities across the United States as well as countries further afield. In fact, the first shipment of building materials arrived before the final building was put out. These photographs taken in 1871 (LEFT) and 1872 show new structures rapidly rising from the ashes.

Grant Park was formed from landfill and rubble cleared from the burned district in the years following the Great Fire (as seen in the picture to the left). The twenty-three-mile park runs along the edge of Lake Michigan the length Chicago and was originally known as Lake Park until renamed in honor of President Ulysses S. Grant in 1901. The remaining photographs shows the ornate Buckingham Fountain, the park's centerpiece, which was built in 1927 in memory of the donor,s brother. The older photo (below) dates from soon after its construction while the color shot is the fountain lit up at night in modern Chicago.

Buckingham Fountain — Grant Park
Chicago

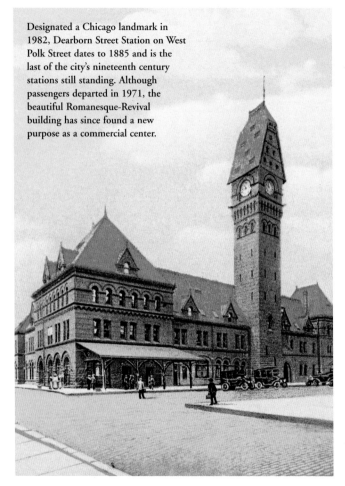

Designated a Chicago landmark in 1982, Dearborn Street Station on West Polk Street dates to 1885 and is the last of the city's nineteenth century stations still standing. Although passengers departed in 1971, the beautiful Romanesque-Revival building has since found a new purpose as a commercial center.

LEFT: Designed by William LeBaron Jenney using his revolutionary steel frame technique, the Home Insurance Building of 1885 is generally regarded as the world's first modern skyscraper. Before it was demolished in 1931, the tower rose 138 feet on South LaSalle Street.

RIGHT: As Chicago boomed, fortunes were made and the wealthy lavished their money on opulent new homes. From about 1880 onward Astor Street, running south from North Avenue to West Division Street, became the fashionable place to live. A Chicago landmark since 1975, the street contains many superb works of architecture.

LEFT: Built between 1880 and 1894, the Pullman Historic District owes its existence to George M. Pullman who decided to create a model community around his railroad car factory rather than manufacture within the city limits. Twelve miles south of central Chicago, Pullman and his architect, Nathan F. Barrett, constructed a carefully landscaped town with every modern convenience and civic amenity. The row houses and apartments were leased to workers in the Pullman Palace Car Company at a profit.

RIGHT: A testament to refined living in late-eighteenth century Chicago and the taste and sophistication of its original owners, the Glessner House was built in 1885–86 by Henry Hobson Richardson and exquisitely decorated by John and Frances Glessner according to the principles of the Arts and Crafts movement. Like so many Chicago buildings, the house would exert an enormous influence on domestic architecture, though at the time other residents along Prairie Avenue reviled its departure from traditional design.

LEFT: Built between 1885 and 1888, The Rookery at 209 South LaSalle Street is one of the finest works of John Root of Burnham & Root and was named for the pigeons that roosted in the temporary buildings that were erected here after the Great Fire. The lobby was remodeled by Frank Lloyd Wright between 1905 and 1907.

RIGHT: A tribute to the combined skills of engineer Dankmar Adler and the creative force of Louis Sullivan, the superbly proportioned and ornamented Auditorium Building, which housed a hotel, offices, and a 4,300 seat theater, was the tallest structure in the city on its completion in 1889 and also the largest ever to incorporate electric lighting and air-conditioning.

Frank Lloyd Wright's Chicago

Frank Lloyd Wright arrived in Chicago at the age of twenty with the dream of becoming an architect. Having worked briefly for Joseph Lyman Silsbee, he soon joined the firm of Adler & Sullivan and became a devoted follower and friend of Louis Sullivan. In 1893, however, Wright established his own office, working out of the home and studio in Oak Park that he referred to as his "laboratory" and which reflects many of his early ideas. Wright quickly found work in a city that was eager to sponsor innovative architecture and today Chicago remains the richest in the buildings of the man who became the United States' foremost architect, and gave the nation its first home-grown architectural style.

The Frank Lloyd Wright Home and Studio in the Chicago suburb of Oak Park was Wright's residence and, latterly, his workplace between 1889 and 1909. Here he raised six children with his first wife (he would eventually create a scandal by running away with the wife of a client) and tested out many of his groundbreaking ideas. The building is full of novel spaces, such as a barrel vaulted playroom and octagonal library and is also full of Wright-designed furniture. A perfectionist who believed in creating every aspect of each building, Wright was even known to design dresses for client's wives.

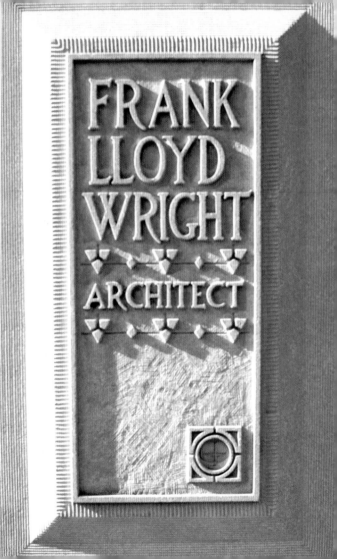

LEFT AND RIGHT: Located just outside the University of Chicago campus, the Robie House, completed in 1910, is the culmination of Wright's Prairie House ideas, and one of the most important pieces of architecture in the country. A complete departure from the European modes of architecture that had previously provided the basis of all American domestic design, it began a new era of modern architecture and is considered to be one of Wright's masterpieces.

LEFT AND BELOW: Unity Temple in Oak Park was a source of great pride for Wright as it showcased an "entirely new architecture."

Completed in 1908, the church was constructed using an innovative method of reinforced poured concrete.

The Ward-Willits House, in the Highland Park suburb, is another excellent example of Prairie House architecture.

ABOVE AND RIGHT: Located in the South Side, in the Hyde Park area, the University of Chicago was founded in 1890 with a donation from John D. Rockefeller and built on land given by Marshall Field. It welcomed its first 594 students in 1892. Today, it is widely regarded as one of the world's finest seats of learning and research, boasting more Nobel Prize laureates among its staff, alumni, and researchers than any other university in the nation. Its campus features the designs of many noted architects, including eighteen buildings by Henry Ives Cobb.

LEFT: Located at 53, West Jackson Boulevard, the Monadnock Building is an architectural curiosity that heralded a new age in building techniques. The northern part of the building was completed under Burnham & Root in 1891 and owes its construction to traditional methods, its sixteen floors being supported by load bearing walls that are six feet thick at the base of the building. The southern half of the building, however, was built by Holabird & Roche between 1891 and 1893 using the new technology of steel-framing.

The World's Columbian Exposition of 1893

The greatest World's Fair of its age, the World's Columbian Exposition had a huge cultural impact in a nation that was struggling to come to terms with the changes wrought by industrialization, electricity, mass immigration, and the shift from a rural to city-based economy. In celebrating the 400th anniversary of Columbus's discovery of the Americas, it also celebrated America itself, its innovations and successes, and helped define a modern nation through exhibits that were instructional, commercial, and fun. In all, over twenty-seven million people from across the country and around the world visited Chicago from May to October that year and found there an incredible complex of Classically-inspired buildings filled with the wonders of the age.

RIGHT: One of the first sights to greet visitors would have been the fair's Administration Building, a magnificent domed building by New York's Richard M. Hunt.

FAR RIGHT: Covering 633 acres of the specially created Jackson Park, the awe-inspiring white exposition buildings were designed by some of the United States' greatest architects, including Charles McKim, Richard Morris Hunt, Henry Ives Cobb, and Louis Sullivan, all under the supervision of Chicago's own Daniel Burnham. The park itself was landscaped by the famous Frederick Law Olmstead.

LEFT: The Palace of Mechanic Arts, close to the entrance of the fair, showcased every kind of mechanical innovation from around the world within its halls. The building also contained the machinery that provided power to the rest of the fairground.

RIGHT: One of the most popular attractions was the first ever Ferris Wheel, designed by George W. Ferris of Pittsburgh. For fifty cents (twice the price of admission to the fair), fairgoers could be travel around two revolutions of the wheel to a height of 264 feet.

A bird's eye view over the exposition.

LEFT: Founded in 1879, the Art Institute of Chicago is now housed in one of the few remaining buildings of the 1893 World's Columbian Exposition. With a collection that spans a huge variety of unique artistic artifacts from around the world, the growth of the institute represented the city's burgeoning cultural maturity and sophistication.

RIGHT: This photograph shows the lively produce market in Haymarket Square in 1893. To the right is a monument erected in 1889, dedicated to the policemen who lost their lives in the Haymarket Riot of 1886, during which an unknown anarchist detonated a bomb at a labor rally. Seven men who had no connection with the crime were later sentenced to death.

NEXT PAGE: Lake Street looking east from Clark around 1893, a time when the city was at the peak of its prosperity. The streets are lined with businesses—a new Spring Suit can be bought for $9.90—and evidence of Chicago's diverse cultural make up is apparent in the names above store fronts, such as M. Griesheimer & Co.

One of Chicago's finest early high-rise buildings, the 186-foot Chicago Stock Exchange building was designed by Frank Lloyd Wright's mentor Louis Sullivan and completed in 1894. Sadly, now demolished, parts of the building have been preserved. The trading room was reconstructed at the Art Institute of Chicago, while this arch from the main entrance can be found at Columbus and Monroe.

LEFT: The importance of the Reliance Building to modern architecture (and perhaps especially to the character of modern Chicago) cannot be underrated. It is to this building that all the glass-clad, soaring skyscrapers of today can trace their ancestry. The revolutionary fourteen-storey tower was constructed using the steel frame pioneered by Jenney, but utilized more confidently to allow an exterior almost entirely devoted to windows. The original design was by John Root, though work was completed under Charles Atwood after Root died in 1891. The Reliance Building opened in 1895.

RIGHT: The Marquette Building at 140 South Dearborn Street owes its elegant exterior to architectural firm of Holabird & Roche and its name to the French Jesuit Jacques Marquette who explored the Chicago area during the winter of 1674-75. Light and airy within, it is beautifully decorated with Tiffany mosaics and bronze sculptures depicting animals, Native-Americans, and pioneers. It was built in 1895.

One of the brightest gems in a city that is an architectural treasure trove, the Carson Pirie Scott and Company Building is another work by Louis Sullivan and dates to 1899. This enormously influential architectural masterpiece features cast-iron work around the first two floors, within which the architect's initials can be found. The building perfectly demonstrates Sullivan's philosophy that "form follows function," an ethic that he would pass on to his most famous student, Frank Lloyd Wright.

LEFT: Chicago's architecture did not just encompass grand public buildings and skyscrapers. By the mid-1800s the city's middle-class residential streets, which spread rapidly as people and wealth poured into the city, were increasingly characterized by new row houses.

RIGHT: By the beginning of the twentieth century, State Street was touted as the busiest street in the world. As this 1903 photograph, looking north from Madison, shows, it is not difficult to understand why.

After long delays and building problems, the first service on Chicago's elevated railway, or the "L" as it came to be known, began on Christmas day 1899. The black and white 1907 photograph shows cars traveling on the tracks above Wabash Avenue. Today, the "L" is still a much-loved part of the city's infrastructure.

LEFT: The successor to the Galena &
Chicago Union Railroad was the
Chicago & Northwestern Railway,
which bought Chicago's first railroad
along with many other companies
and also extended the network of
tracks. At the time it was the biggest
operator on the Midwest. This
photograph shows the Madison Street
Entrance to the company's passenger
terminal in 1912.

RIGHT: Older than any other
building on "Magnificent Mile,"
Fourth Presbyterian Church opened
its doors in 1914. Designed by Ralph
Adams Cram, the church has seen the
neighborhood rise around it.

Chicago's waterfront in 1913 shows a skyline that is beginning to reach higher, though the buildings here will be dwarfed by those that are only a few years in the future.

CHICAGO'S

TER FRONT

Copyrighted 1913
by
Kaufmann Weimer & Fabry Co.
Chicago

Wrigley Field was built in 1914 and named for the Cubs, who played here from 1916 onward. In fact, it was not until 1927 that the ballpark was renamed in honor of new owner William Wrigley. The black and white photograph shows fans packed into the park for a Cubs game in July 1927, while the modern photo shows how little the park has changed.

Chicago Grows Up: 1915–45

As the city matured, this period saw the construction of some of Chicago's most revered buildings, such as the Wrigley Building and Tribune Tower.

Chicago Grows Up: 1915–45

It was during this period that the city began to look as we would recognize it today. Daniel Burnham's 1909 Plan of Chicago began to bear fruit in the shape of Wacker Drive, a straightened river, parks, recreation grounds, and new transport systems, while many of the Chicago's best-known buildings were constructed: the Wrigley Building, Merchandise Mart, and Tribune Tower to name just three. Though Chicago continued to grow through war and peacetime, its population increases slowed somewhat. Now, however, a new contingent of immigrants arrived. This time the Great Migration came not from Europe, but from the fields of the South as African-Americans flocked to enjoy the employment opportunities that Chicago offered when World War I got underway. While the city that had been founded by an African-American had long enjoyed a dynamic black community, now its number swelled and so too did Chicago's musical scene as the city made Jazz and blues music its own. The music would become the city's soundtrack during the Prohibition era during which Chicago, perhaps more than any other American city, flouted the ban on booze. Between the wars, Chicago also hosted its second World's Fair, the 1933 Century of Progress that celebrated the centenary of Chicago's incorporation. True to its traditions as the transport hub of America, the Municipal Airport (later renamed Midway), which opened in 1927, was by the end of World War II not only the busiest airport in the United States, but the busiest airport in the world.

While Chicago was developing into distinctive neighborhoods, often based on ethnic background, as early as the 1850s it was during the Great Migration and the increased employment brought by World War I that a band south of the Loop become a predominantly African-American neighborhood. Sadly, the influx caused racial tension that flared into rioting in 1919. Nevertheless, over the following years the South Side proved a coherent and resilient community that nurtured great musicians, particularly blues players and gospel singers such as Mahalia Jackson. Still a great center of African-American culture, the South Side even fields its own major league baseball team.

A view along Lake Shore Drive in about 1915.

BELOW, RIGHT, AND OVERLEAF: At 3,000 feet, Navy Pier was the longest pier in the world when it opened in 1916. Originally intended as a dual purpose recreation area and shipping dock, the pier was originally a popular place for family outings, but declined during the twenties and thirties as movie houses opened, the Great Depression deepened, and transportation by truck began to replace shipping. Serving as a naval training base during World War II, it was later used by the University of Illinois. Designated a Chicago landmark in the seventies, at the end of the following decade a $150 million budget was set aside for restoration and renewal, and Navy Pier opened again in its most recent incarnation in 1994. Now teeming with parks, gardens, rides, and attractions it is again one of Chicago's most popular entertainment destinations.

LEFT: Chicago's most notable example of Italianate design, the Drake Hotel is beautifully situated at the northern end of "Magnificent Mile" with views over Lake Michigan. Opened in 1920, for many years it vied with the Palmer House as Chicago's most opulent hotel.

RIGHT: Located at the southern end of Magnificent Mile, the Wrigley Building rises over the Chicago River. Completed in 1924 (two and a half centuries after Jacques Marquette and Louis Joliet arrived at this very spot) and built to house the chewing gum company of William Wrigley, Jr., the building occupies an unusually shaped building plot. It was modeled on the shape of Seville Cathedral's Giralda Tower, while the ornamentation is Beaux Arts style.

The city's oldest remaining theater and an incredible confection of interior design, the Chicago Theatre is also one of its most famous sites. Despite being an irreplacable part of the cityscape, the building was scheduled for demolition in 1986 until saved by the Chicago Theater Restoration Associates. Originally a movie house that opened on October, 26, 1921, with Norma Talmadge in "The Sign on the Door," the theater now stages shows and has starred many of the world's brightest acting and singing talents.

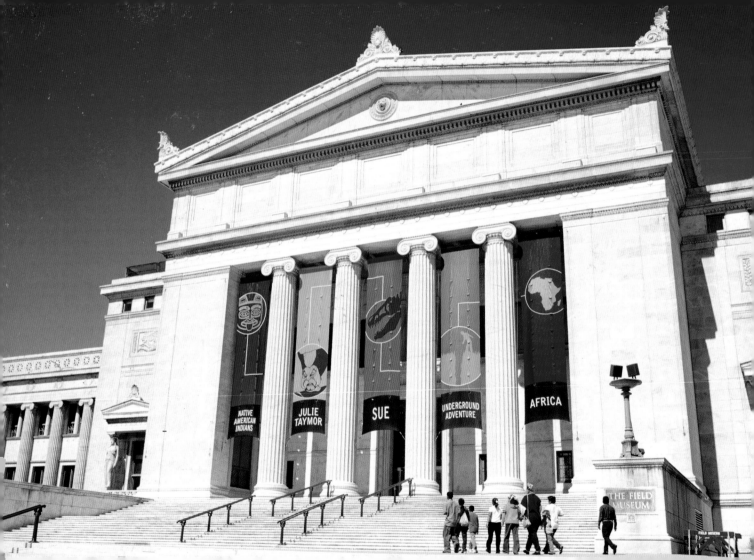

LEFT, RIGHT AND OVERLEAF: One of Chicago's most highly regarded institutions, the Field Museum originally opened in 1894 in the Palace of Fine Arts building on the site of the Columbian Exposition, but moved here in 1921 when that building proved too small. As the museum's name suggests, it owes its existence to a donation from Marshall Field and now has one of the world's finest collections, encompassing human antiquities, botanical exhibits, and zoological specimens including a number of dinosaur fossils.

GREAT · WALL
CHINA

The winners of a competition run by the *Chicago Tribune* in 1922 to design the world's most beautiful office building were New York's Howell & Hood. The resulting Gothic-inspired skyscraper, topped with ornate flying butresses, was completed three years later and is now one of Chicago's best-loved landmarks. At ground level around its outer walls are imbedded rocks and masonry from other famous sites and buildings around the world, as well as a piece of moon rock.

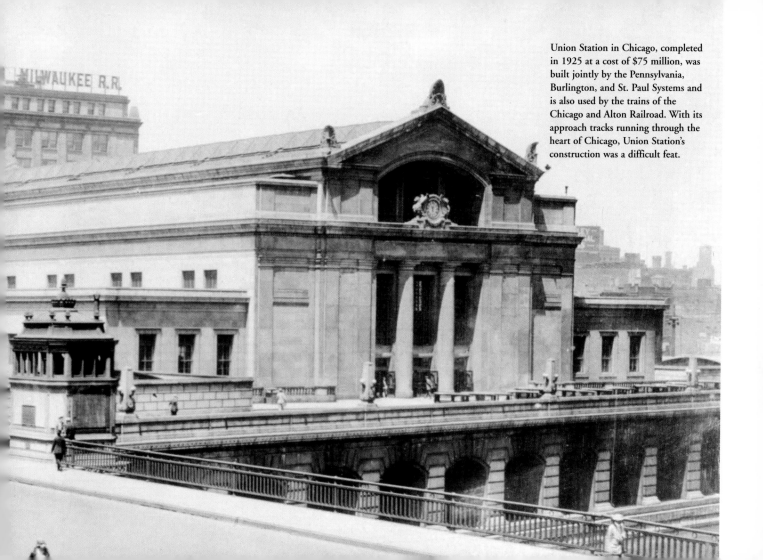

Union Station in Chicago, completed in 1925 at a cost of $75 million, was built jointly by the Pennsylvania, Burlington, and St. Paul Systems and is also used by the trains of the Chicago and Alton Railroad. With its approach tracks running through the heart of Chicago, Union Station's construction was a difficult feat.

The Plan of Chicago

LEFT: Daniel Burnham's Michican Avenue Bridge, which opened for traffic in 1926. As proposed by the plan, the bridge provided additional access to North Michigan Avenue, which resulted in the street's evolution into one of Chicago's busiest districts.

RIGHT: The plan also called for the straightening of the Chicago River between Polk and Eighteenth streets. On completion in 1930, the removal of the river's natural bend allowed the expansion of the business district to the south.

This grand scheme, the first ever to envision urban planning on such a vast scale, set out a seemlessly integrated city with wide avenues, numerous parks, and recreational facilities served by excellent transportation. While Chicago never fully realized the 1909 vision of Daniel Burnham and his collaborator Edward Bennett, the plan wielded an enormous influence over the shape that the city would take as it grew over the decades to come. It directly inspired the creation of many of the city's public parks as well as the Field Museum and improvements to transportation systems. Its legacies are to be found everywhere in the modern city and its environment.

LEFT AND ABOVE: Another integral part of modern Chicago that owes its existence to the 1909 Plan of Chicago is Wacker Drive, which was proposed by Burnham and Bennett to improve Chicago's traffic flow. The idea for a double-decker roadway was championed by the chairman of the Chicago Plan Commission, Charles H. Wacker, and named for him on completion in 1926.

The caption for the drawing notes that it is the plan for Wacker Drive as it will appear when it is lined with buildings. The drive formerly housed the world's largest produce market, which was moved to the West side of the city, to make room for this new boulevard.

LEFT: The Palmer House Hotel (now the Palmer House Hilton) is the third hotel on this site to be built by Chicago magnate Potter Palmer. The first was open just thirteen days before being burned down in the Great Fire. This photograph shows the grand lobby of the most recent, which was built between 1924 and 1927.

RIGHT: Completed in 1930 and designated a Chicago Landmark in 1977, the Chicago Board of Trade Building, at the end of LaSalle Street, is a superb example of Art Deco design by Holabird & Root.

LEFT: Shedd Aquarium, with its curved glass wall that provides magnificent views out onto Lake Michigan, was completed in 1930 and named for city businessman and philanthropist John G. Shedd, who funded the building. The aquarium has been a favorite with Chicagoans and tourists since, and houses a vast collection of aquatic wildlife, from sharks and dolphins to rare amphibians.

RIGHT: Built on an artificial island to the east of the Field Museum (since joined to the shore), the Adler Planetarium was the first of its kind in the Western Hemisphere and the brainchild of another wealthy Chicago businessman; Max Adler. The result of his generosity was this amazing building, designed by Ernest Grunsfeld and opened in 1930. The planetarium houses a collection of historical astronomical artifacts, which was originally donated by Adler and has been added to ever since. It now also contains theaters that recreate a journey through the solar system and beyond in stunning 3-D. As an interesting historical footnote, the architect's grandson, John Grunsfeld, became a NASA astronaut who completed the family's journey into space in 1999.

As the first section of Wacker Drive was completed, Marshall Field & Co. revealed their plans for this Art Deco Chicago behemoth. Billed as the "Biggest Building in the World," Merchandise Mart was designed by Graham, Anderson, Probst & White and opened on May 5, 1930, only a few short months after the beginning of the Great Depression. Intended as a single wholesale outlet to replace the company's various interests across the city, Marshall Field's was financially forced to reduce its own space in the building soon after completion. The building was bought by Joseph P. Kennedy, Sr. in 1945 and was managed by the Kennedy family for half a century.

Held on 427 acres immediately south of downtown on the shore of Lake Michigan in 1933, Chicago's second World's Fair was the Century of Progress International Exposition, which honored the centenary of the city's incorporation as a city. Taking its theme from scientific innovation, the fair proved so popular that it was opened again in 1934.

ABOVE: Originally known as Leif Erickson Drive, the downtown stretch of Lake Shore Drive (known as "LSD" to locals) was opened in 1937 and renamed in 1945. The current stretch of roadway was rebuilt between 1982 and 1986. Lined by upscale neighborhoods, such as Gold Coast, Old Town, and Lincoln Park, and also running through miles of parkland on the edge of Lake Michigan to the south of the river, Lake Shore Drive is a scenic ride as well as a vital urban artery.

RIGHT: Chicago has a reputation for undertaking difficult engineering problems, and one of most problematic was the creation of its subway system. The main challenge facing construction workers was the soft clay beneath the city that had once made its streets so notoriously muddy. Nevertheless, the subway was built in just seven years, and without a single cave-in. It opened on October 17, 1943.

An atmospheric Chicago street scene
taken in 1940 from beneath the lines
of the elevated railway.

The City of Towers:
1945–Today

Chicago's skyline at sunset reflected in the *Cloud Gate* sculpture in Millennium Park.

The City of Towers: 1945–Today

Having pioneered the skyscraper, Chicago went on to experiment with different styles and materials. The result is one of the most dramatic, tallest, and most recognizable skylines in the world. In fact, at the time of going to press, the city has 1,558 high rise buildings with more due to start construction. Outside of the business district though, Chicago's population growth slowed and then reversed after peaking in the 1950s, with people moving out to the suburbs in the fifties and leaving behind a city in need of renovation. Nevertheless, under Mayor Richard J. Daley and his successors, Chicago has continued to invest in its infrastructure, architecture, parks, and cultural institutions with the result that it is now one of the most attractive and liveable of the world's large cities, a fact that has seen the population begin to increase again since the nineties. Today, Chicago retains its position as transport center of the United States. One of the best-planned and organized cities in the world, it is an incredibly diverse place that offers every kind of artistic and cultural experience that can be imagined, from intimate lakeside cafes and restaurants to world-class museums and galleries. It is a city where decades of changing architectural styles sit comfortably alongside one another and an optimistic, pioneering spirit still exists.

Following the end of World War II, Chicago moved its reputation as the transport hub of America into the skies. Initially it was the Municipal Airport (Midway) that was the star performer, but by 1962 all operations were transferred to O'Hare, which had begun as a small airfield built on Orchard Field in 1946. The airport was renamed in 1949 after heroic navy pilot Lieutenant Edward O'Hare. Today, the airport handles in excess of seventy million passengers each year. For many people visiting Chicago their first taste of the city is the incredible 744-foot-long neon sculpture at Terminal One. Called *The Sky's The Limit*, it was designed in 1987 by Michael Hayden.

ABOVE: While Chicago's skyline was beginning to take its modern shape by the mid 1950s when this photograph was taken, it had yet to construct the soaring towers that would see it rival, and then overtake New York as the home of the nation's tallest buildings.

RIGHT: Known as the "corncob," the two towers of Marina City at 300 North State Street owe their unusual appearance to Betrand Goldberg Associates and opened in 1967. To the right of the photograph is Mies van der Rohe's famous IBM Building, built in the International Style and dating to 1971.

LEFT: Built in 1968, Lake Point Tower was the first commission awarded to its architects and was based on a 1922 design by Mies van der Rohe. Located at the base of Navy Pier, the building is designed so that none of the residents can see through the windows of any other apartment, and all have a view out over Lake Michigan.

RIGHT: The first building outside of New York City to top 1,000 feet, the John Hancock Center, at 875 North Michigan Avenue, was completed in 1969 and was at the time the third tallest building in the US. Still one of Chicago's defining landmarks, the tower, which is crossed by X-shaped steel braces all the way up its 1,127 feet, was designed by Bruce Graham and Fazlur Khan of Skidmore, Owings, and Merrill.

LEFT: Contrasting with Chicago's two landmark black towers, Aon Center is a simple white granite-clad skyscraper with vertical stripes of black windows. Built in 1973, at 1,136 feet Aon Center is actually the tallest building in the world if antenna, finials, and other ornamentation are discounted.

RIGHT: Another of Mies van der Rohe's Chicago projects is 1974's Federal Center, which comprises three stark, International Style civic buildings around a central courtyard. The curious sculpture that is the sole occupant of the plaza is called *Flamingo* and was crafted by Alexander Calder.

Structurally, the world's tallest building from its completion in 1974 until that title was taken by Petronas Towers in Kuala Lumpar in 1996, Sears Tower measures 1,451 feet and consists of nine towers clustered together to make up the distinctive shape. Encased in black anodized aluminum panels with bronze tinted windows, the sleek building includes one of the world's fastest elevators and is so high that workers on higher floors have been known to suffer motion sickness induced by the skyscraper's sway. Like its neighbor, the John Hancock Center, Sears Tower was designed by Bruce Graham and Fazlur Khan.

The award-winning 333 Wacker Drive is a beautifully simple glass-walled skyscraper with a curved façade that follows the contour of a curve in the Chicago River. Completed in 1985, this was the first ever skyscraper designed by a team now world-famous for its high-rise buildings, Kohn Pedersen Fox Associates PC.

RIGHT: Housing government offices, shops, galleries, and restauranta the postmodern James R. Thompson Center was designed by Helmut Jahn as a space for public office that would be as transparent as possible and close the gap between government and citizens. The 1985 building is entirely clad in glass and features a vast and awe-inspiring atrium.

LEFT: 900 North Michigan Avenue is a 1989 postmodern extravaganza incorporating Art Deco and Palladian influences. One of Chicago's many modern skyscrapers it is also one of the tallest and is often referred to as the Bloomingdale's Building as the department store has large premises here.

RIGHT: Although the title of America's second city has passed to Los Angeles, modern Chicago remains the transportation hub of America and the financial heart of the Midwest.

Millennium Park

Almost twenty-five years in the making, Chicago's Millennium Park has transformed an area that was once occupied by railroad tracks into one of the most spectacular city parks in the world, complete with incredible feats of architecture and works of art. A park devoted to the performing arts was originally proposed in 1977, but it was not until 1997 when Mayor Richard M. Daley became interested that the project began to make serious headway. Under the mayor, and with the involvement of architect Frank Gehry, the landscaping of the area was transformed into one of the most ambitious construction projects ever undertaken within the city.

LEFT: Designed by Frank Gehry the Jay Pritzker Pavilion provides the park with a concert venue and a startling architectural masterpiece, all in one. The trellis above the lawn houses a state-of-the-art sound system that replicates the acoustic quality of an indoor venue.

RIGHT: One of the park's most popular installations is *Cloud Gate* by Anish Kapoor. The highly polished stainless steel sculpture forms a low arch in which the city's famous skyline and the sky are reflected. Visitors can walk beneath and see themselves reflected also.

The BP Bridge, also designed by Frank Gehry, is a meandering walkway that connects Millennium Park to Daley Centennial Plaza and also gives pedestrians superb views of the city's skyline.

Skyscrapers tower above the Chicago River in the business district. Today's city is revered as a crucible of architectural experimentation. Indeed, the innovations in building techniques that Chicago has pioneered have shaped the look of modern cities around the globe.

Modern visitors find that one of the best ways to view Chicago's architectural marvels is by tour boat along the Chicago River.

At the beginning of the third millennium, Chicago has one of the most famous skylines in the world, with more incredible, and taller, buildings planned for the future.

Picture Credits